The Devil's Chimney, near Ullenwood

Footnotes on a Landscape – 2

COTSWOLD PLACE-NAMES

A CONCISE DICTIONARY

DAVID WHITTAKER

wavestone
press

Dedicated to
Penny and Alice
(the bookends of my life)
for keeping me propped up

COTSWOLD PLACE-NAMES: A CONCISE DICTIONARY

ISBN: 0954519426

WAVESTONE PRESS
6 ROCHESTER PLACE, CHARLBURY, OXON OX7 3SF, UK
Tel: 01608-811435
Email: wavestone@btinternet.com
Web: www.wavestonepress.co.uk

Acknowledgements:
This dictionary would have been inconceivable without the pioneering work of previous scholars. In particular Eilert Ekwall, A.H. Smith and Margaret Gelling. I am humbly indebted to the English Place-Name Society at the University of Nottingham for providing such outstanding volumes of knowledge to be mined. Their web address is: www.nottingham.ac.uk/research/EPNS/
    Any errors in the text are down to this plebeian author's inadequate application by way of research.
    With gratitude to the anonymous illustrator of the map used in this book. At the time of going to press all attempts to locate them to seek their permission for its use were unsuccessful.

Front endpaper: Broadway Tower.
Rear endpaper: St Peter's, Winchcombe.

As ever, a big thanks to Keith Rigley for angelic technical guidance.
Printed by Information Press, Eynsham, Oxon.

CONTENTS

Map of the Cotswold Area

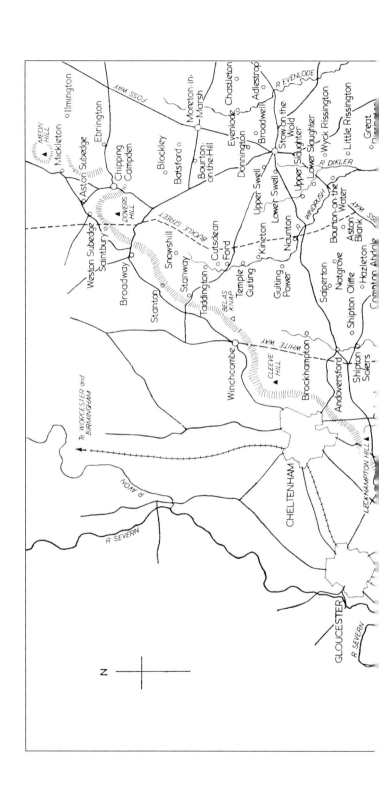

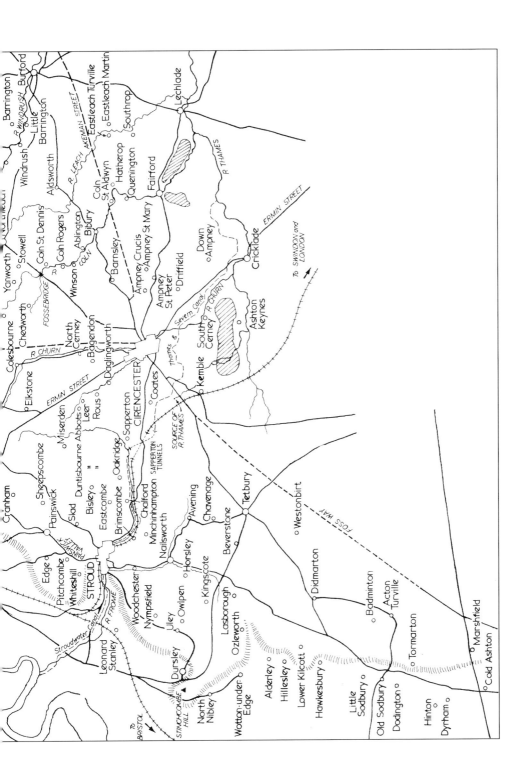

Barrington

Little Barrington

Windrush

R. WINDRUSH

Burford

Aldsworth

AKEMAN STREET

Eastleach Turville

Eastleach Martin

Southrop

Lechlade

R. LEACH

Coln St Dennis

Coln Rogers

Ablington

Bibury

Coln St Aldwyn

Hatherop

Quenington

Fairford

Stowell

R.

Winson

COLN

Barnsley

R. THAMES

Yanworth

Chedworth

FOSSEBRIDGE

Ampney Crucis

Ampney St Mary

Driffield

Down Ampney

Colesbourne

R. CHURN

North Cerney

Bagendon

Ampney St Peter

Thames & Severn Canal

South Cerney

R. CHURN

Ashton Keynes

Cricklade

ERMIN STREET

To SWINDON and LONDON

Elkstone

ERMIN STREET

Daglingworth

CIRENCESTER

Coates

Kemble

Miserden

Leer

Rous

Sapperton

Duntisbourne Abbots

SOURCE OF R. THAMES

Shepscombe

Bisley

Oakridge

SAPPERTON TUNNELS

Cranham

Painswick

Slad

Eastcombe

Brimscombe

Chalford

Minchinhampton

Nailsworth

Avening

Chavenage

Tetbury

Westonbirt

FOSS WAY

Edge

Pitchcombe

Whiteshill

PAINSWICK VALLEY

STROUD

Horsley

Kingscote

Beverstone

Didmarton

Badminton

Acton Turville

Leonard Stanley

R. FROME

Woodchester

Nympsfield

Owlpen

Uley

Stroudwater Canal

Dursley

Lasborough

Ozleworth

Tormarton

Marshfield

STINCHCOMBE HILL

North Nibley

Wotton-under-Edge

Alderley

Hillesley

Lower Kilcott

Hawkesbury

Little Sodbury

Old Sodbury

Dodington

Hinton

Dyrham

Cold Ashton

TO BRISTOL

7

Introduction

Where are the Cotswolds?

This simple question is a lot trickier to answer than might be imagined. According to one broad definition, Massingham in *Cotswold Country*, it is the name given to a uniform, oolitic limestone belt running from Dorset to Yorkshire ('oolite' comes from the Greek *oon* 'egg' and *lithos* 'stone' and is a rock made up of granules of calcium carbonate pressed together like the roe of a fish). But the heart of the Cotswolds is made up of high ground and its approaches centred mainly in the eastern part of Gloucestershire with some overlap in Oxfordshire, Worcestershire, Warwickshire and Wiltshire. There is no clear borderline, but for the purposes of this book some boundary had to be introduced to prevent the project sprawling out of control. The Hadfield's important book *The Cotswolds* came to the rescue and provided just such a useful frontier. They separate the Cotswolds from the Bath hills, the Berkshire downs, the Oxfordshire hills and Northamptonshire uplands; while Gloucester and Cheltenham are in the Vale of Gloucester. Their delineation adheres to a 40 mile long escarpment south of and parallel to the Severn valley from Wotton-under-Edge to the bluffs above Ilmington north of Chipping Camden, spreading south to Didmarton and Hawkesbury and to the east near Burford and Chipping Norton. Though much of the surrounding area can claim Cotswold influence, particularly in building, it cannot claim to be Cotswold (the Oxfordshire Cotswolds is a more recent label and they will be treated in a planned companion volume *Oxfordshire Place-Names*).

The line had to be drawn somewhere and it is the nature of boundaries to exclude as well as include; I apologise to those who feel unfairly placed on the wrong side of this definition. A selection of towns and places surrounding the Cotswolds has been added in an appendix by way of a compromise.

What's in a name?

As we speed around the countryside or sit in traffic jams, cocooned in our tin cans, we take the names on road signs and maps very much for granted. We live with them all our lives, they've become a part of our daily vocabulary and we rarely relate them to the surrounding environment; but that is where they have their roots. It's easy to overlook the fact that they can be a rich source of social and natural history, archaeology and topography. They are a kind of linguistic fossil helping to articulate the changes that have occurred to the landscape for well over a thousand years.

A serious study of place-names requires some widely informed detective work and there are many pitfalls for the unwary toponymist (from the Greek *topos* 'place' and *onoma* 'name'). It is important to remember that place-names were spoken long before they were written down. They were a kind of oral map for, amongst other things, guiding people across an often hostile terrain between settlements, indicating the ease of access, or otherwise, across various topographical features particularly rivers and floodplains; they also located springs, forests, tracks, clearings, ploughland, pastures, marshland, flora and fauna and could even give some clues to the weather in an area. Gradually they got transcribed for a variety of reasons including estate and land surveying, ecclesiastical records, deeds, tithes, charters, taxes and as maps became more widespread. Spellings were phonetic and probably didn't take into account dialectical variations. This is especially true of that monumental chronicle the Domesday Book (1086), when names were collected by Norman-French civil servants who would have found the accents and dialects of local people very foreign indeed. The problem is compounded by spellings becoming further corrupted over the centuries. Therefore beware: what seems an obvious meaning from the spelling of a place can prove to be something quite different.

Philologists, dealing with the structure and development of language, have painstakingly pieced together likely meanings for most place-names; nevertheless puzzles remain and, erring on the side of caution, the words 'probably' and 'possibly' recur throughout this text. Research by the English Place-name Society and intrepid individuals is ongoing and the academic debate over meanings can sometimes be very contentious. A concise dictionary such as this cannot provide the scope to discuss what are often highly technical issues, much bigger books already exist and can be found listed in the bibliography.

Names within names

Many place-names refer to a personal, family or tribal name. In most cases little or nothing is known about the Anglo-Saxon celebrities who were worthy enough to lend their names to often large areas of land (e.g., Cotswolds, Andoversford, Dursley); the presence of whole tribes can also be seen (Cirencester, Wychwood). Much later with the Norman conquest came the feudal families whose names became affixed to the place were they held their manor (Eastleach Turville, Shipton Solers, Frampton Mansell). Certain individuals also lent their names to a place or feature in their possession (Ball's Green, France Lynch, Hetty Pegler's Tump) while others make an appearance as part of local folklore (Betty's Grave).

A note about 'bottoms'

There is a proliferation of 'bottoms' in and around the Cotswolds (Waste Bottom, Cobbler's Bottom, Hedgley Bottom). They are mainly modern additions to place-names (inserted in an *a posteriori* sense, perhaps) and have therefore not been included in the listing of elements (OE *bytme*, *botm*). The term describes a flat alluvial area, usually moist and often flooded and is generally the lowest part of a valley.

The format of this book

All of the towns, villages and notable features (including the odd) on the Ordnance Survey Explorer series (1:25000 scale) are listed except for farm and field names which could well constitute a separate study.

Here is a typical example of an entry:

BURFORD
Beorgford 752, Bureford DB. Ford by a fortified place. [burh, ford]

The place-name in bold is followed, in italics, by the earliest recorded spelling with date (if known) and Domesday Book spelling (if there is one). The most likely definition follows. Finally the place-name elements are placed in square brackets. In a few instances several spellings have been supplied (Cotswolds, Cirencester, Thames).

Abbreviations

c.   century
ca.   circa
DB   Domesday Book 1086
EPNS   English Place-Name Society
ME   Middle English
ModE   Modern English
OE   Old English
OFr   Old French
p. name   personal name
r. name   river name
t. name   tribe name

GLOSSARY

Glossary of place-name elements in the text; all Old English unless otherwise stated (the letters þ and ð, called *thorn* and *eth* respectively, have been modernised as *th*):

āc   oak-tree

æsc   ash-tree

æwelm   river spring, source of river

ald   old

alor   alder

amore   bird, possibly bunting

bæc-hūs   bake-house

bagga   animal, possibly badger

banke   ME sloping bank

bedd   plot of ground

bēl   fire, beacon

beofor   beaver

beorg   hill or mound

bere   barley

blæc   black

bōc   beech-tree

bōc-land   land granted by charter

boga   bow, arch, bend

box   box-tree

brād   broad, spacious

braec   thicket

brēmel   bramble

bridd   bird

brōc   brook or stream

brycg   bridge, marshland causeway

brȳd   bride

bula   bull

burg   burrow

burh   fortified place, stronghold

burna   stream, spring

butt   log, stump, ME 'archery butt'

butte strip of land abutting on a boundary
cald cold
calu bare place
camp field, enclosed piece of land
catt cat, wild cat
cealc chalk
ceastel heap of stones
ceaster Roman station, walled town or villa
ceorl freeman, peasant
cēping market place
cēse cheese, cheese-producing
cirice church
clif cliff, bank
clopp lump, hillock, hill
clympre lump of metal, clod
cnæpp hill top, sharp ascent
cnafa young man, servant
cnēow knee (bend in river or road)
cnoll hill-top, hillock
coccel tares
cocc-scīete glade where woodcock were caught
coninger rabbit warren
corn corn, grain
cot cottage, hut, shelter
cran crane or possibly heron
crȳc hill
cū cow
culcor water hole
cumb coomb, valley
cwēn queen, consort of king
cwene woman
cȳft meeting place
cyne- kingly, royal
cyning king
cȳta kite
denu valley
dīc ditch
dræg drag, slipway, dray
drīf stubble
drit dirt
dūce duck

dūn   hill

dūne   down, below

ēa   river, stream

ēan   lamb

ears   buttocks

ēast   eastern

ecg   edge

ēg   island

ende   end, end of district or estate

fæger   fair, beautiful, pleasant

fearn   fern

feld   open country

fīf   five

ford   ford, shallow place across a stream

foss   ditch

fox   fox

fōl   foul, dirty

geat   hole, opening, gap

gelād   river crossing

grāf   grove, copse

grēote   gravelly place, stream

gyte   pouring forth, flood

hæsel   hazel

hæthen   heathen

hafoc   hawk

halh   nook, corner of land, water-meadow

hālig   holy, sacred

hām   homestead, manor, estate, village

hamm   enclosure, meadow, land in river bend

hangra   wood on steep slope

hār   hoar, grey

hēah   high place

hecg   hedge

hēg   hay

henn   hen, usually water-hen

heorot   hart

herepæth   military road, highway

hīd   hide of land (c. 120 acres)

hlædel   ladel

hlāw   mound or tumulus

hlēp   leap, jumping place, steep declivity

hlīep-geat   leaping gate for deer

hlinc   ridge, bank

hnutu   nut

hnybba   point or tip of hill

hogg   hog

holt   wood thicket

horn   nook, projecting nook of land

hors   horse

horu   filth, dirt

hrēod   reed, rush

hrīsen   growing with or made of brushwood

hrycg   ridge

hunig   honey, sweet

hūs   house

hwit   white, clear, bright

hylda   skinner or butcher

hyll   hyll

hyrcg   ridge

in   in, inner, within

-ing   place characterised by, place belonging to

-ing-   associated with or called after

-inga-   possessive case of -ingas

-ingas   people of, followers of, dwellers at

īw   yew-tree

læcc   stream, bog

lǣfer   rush, reed

lǣssaer   lesser, smaller

landrih   land rights connected with the ownership of an estate

lang   long strip of land

lāwerce or **lāferce**   lark

lēac   leek, garlic

lēah   wood, woodland clearing or glade

leahtric   lettuce

litistere   ME dyer

lȳtel   little

mære   boundary

mann   man

mere   pool

mersc   watery land, marsh

micel   big, great

middel   middle

mōr   moor

munuc   monk

myln   mill

mynecen   nun

næt   wet, moist

neothera   lower

netele   nettle

nīwe   new

north   northern, north

ofer   hill, ridge

ōra   border, margin, bank, edge

ōsle   blackbird

oxa   ox

pæth   path

penn   small enclosure, pen

pēo   insect or parasite

picen   pitchy, pertaining to pitch

pinca   finch or chaffinch

pōl or **pull**   pool, pond

port   town

posa   bag, hollow

prīost   priest

pūca   goblin

pynd   pond

pytt   pit, excavation

quarriere   OF, ME quarry

rā   roe-buck

rand   edge, border, brink

rāw   row (of houses, trees etc.)

reps, **resp**   accusation, inquiry

risc   rush

rodde   rod, slender shoot

ryge   rye

salt   salt

sāpere   soap maker or dealer

scēap   sheep

scearn   dung, muck

scēne   bright

scēot   steep slope

scīr   bright

scrubb   shrub, brushwood

senget   place cleared by burning

seofon   seven

sīde   hill-side

slæd   valley

slōhtre   slough, mire, muddy place

snāw   snow

spōn   wood shavings

stān   stone, rock

sticol   steep

stīg   path

stint   sandpiper or dunlin

stoc   secondary settlement

stocc   tree trunk, log

stōw   place, assembly place, holy place

strǣt   Roman road, paved roads

strōd   marshland overgrown with brushwood

sulh-mann   ploughman

sūth   southern, south

swelle   swelling

swīn   swine, pig

thīof   thief

thicce   thick, dense

thorn   thorn-tree, hawthorn

throp   hamlet, outlying farm

thrūh   water-pipe, conduit

tikil   ME unstable, balancing

trūs   brushwood

tump   ModE dialect for small hillock

tūn   farmstead, enclosure, village, estate

ūle   owl

upp   up, higher up

wæsc   washing place

wæter   water, pool, stream, river

wald   woodland, forest later cleared as open high ground

Walh   Welshman

waste   wasteland (ME, OFr)

weg   way, path, road

wella   well, spring or stream

welm   surging or welling up of water

wulf   wolf

DICTIONARY

ABLINGTON

Eadbaldingtun 855. Farmstead associated with Ēadbald. [p. name, -ing-, tūn]

ADLESTROP

Titlestrop 714, Tedestrop DB. Tǣtel's outlying farmstead. [p. name, throp]

ALDSWORTH

Ealdeswyrthe 1004, Aldeswrde DB. Ald's enclosure. [p. name, worth]

ALDERLEY

Alrelie DB. Woodland clearing of alders. [alor, lēah]

AMBERLEY

Unberleia 1166. Probably woodland clearing of the bunting. [amore, lēah]

AMPNEY CRUCIS, AMPNEY ST MARY, AMPNEY ST PETER, DOWN AMPNEY

Omenie DB, Ameneye Sancte Crucis 1287, Ammeneye Beate Marie 1297, Amenel

Ampney St Peter

Sancti Petri ca. 1275, Dunamenell 1205. Amma's stream (from Ampney Brook). A. C. (Latin *crucis* 'of the cross') dedication is to the Holy Rood Church; A. St M. dedication to the church of the Virgin Mary; A. St P. dedicated to the abbey of St Peter in Gloucester; D. A. most southerly of the Ampneys. [p. name, ēa, dūne]

ANDOVERSFORD
Onnan ford 759. Anna's ford. [p. name, ford]

ARLEBROOK
Arlebroke 1268. Alder brook. [alor, brōc]

ARLINGTON
Ælfredincgtune 1002, Alvredintune DB. Farmstead associated with Alfred. [p. name, -ing-, tūn]

ASHBROOK
Estbroce DB. Land east of the brook. [ēast, brōc]

ASHLEY
Esselie DB. Ash glade or clearing. [æsc, lēah]

ASTON BLANK or COLD ASTON
Eastunæ 8th c., Estone DB. Eastern farmstead, cold or exposed; affix possibly *OFr blanc* 'white, bare'. [ēast, tūn]

ASTON MAGNA, ASTON SUBEDGE
Estone DB. East Farmstead. *Magna* means 'great' to distinguish it from Aston Sub Edge, below the edge or scarp [ēast, tūn, ecg]

AVENING
Æfeningum 896, Aveninge DB. People settled by the River Avon. [r. name, -ingas]

AYLWORTH
Ailwrde DB. Ægel's enclosure. [p. name, worth]

BACCHUS
Backhouse 1824. Bake-house. [bæc-hūs]

BADBROOK
Badbrooke 1609. Bada's brook. [p. name, brōc]

BAGENDON
Benwedene DB. Valley of Bæcga's people. [p. name, -inga-, denu]

BAGPATH
Baggepathe 1174. Possibly badger's track. [bagga, pæth]

BALL'S GREEN
Ballesmede 1438. From the surname 'Ball'.

BARFORD

bereford 852. Ford where barley harvests are transported. [bere, ford]

BARNSLEY

Bearmodeslea ca. 802, Bernesleis DB. Beornmōd's glade or clearing. [p. name, lēah]

BARRINGTON, LITTLE & GREAT

Bernitone DB. Farmstead associated with Beorn. [p. name, -ing-, tūn]

BARTON

Berton 1158. Barley farm, outlying grange where corn is stored. [bere-tūn]

BATSFORD

Bæccesore 727, Beceshore DB. Bæcci's slope. [p. name, ōra]

BATTLESCOMBE

Battlescombe 1609. Probably Baeddel's valley. [p. name, cumb]

BAUNTON

Baudintone DB. Farmstead associated with Balda. [p. name, -ing-, tūn]

BELAS KNAP

Belknap 1361. Beacon hill. [bēl, cnæpp]

BETTY'S GRAVE

Betty's Grove 1796. Several stories exist about a mysterious Betty buried on this spot: maybe a suicide or a poisoner or a witch with a stake driven through her heart or even the Betty who took up a wager to cut a field of hay in a day and on completion dropped down dead.

St Mary's, Bibury

BEVERSTON

Beurestane DB. Beofor's stone or beaver's stone. [p. name or beofor, stān]

BIBURY

Beaganbyrig 8th c., Begeberie DB. Fortified place or stronghold of Bēage. [p. name, burh]

BIDFIELD

Budevilla 1191. Byda's open ground. [p. name, feld]

BIRDLIP

Brydelepe 1221. Bird or bride's leap. [bridd or brīd, hlēp]

BISLEY

Bislege 986, Biselege DB. Bisa's glade or clearing. [p. name, lēah]

BISMORE

Bismore 1609. Bisa's marshy land. [p. name, mōr]

BLACKEMORE COVERT

Blackmore Coppice 1830. Black moor coppice. [blæc, mōr]

BLEAKMOOR

Blackmore 1830. Black moor. [blæc, mōr]

BLEDINGTON

Bladintun DB. Farmstead on River Bladon. [r. name, tūn]

BLEDISLOE

Bliteslau DB. Blith's mound. [p. name, hlāw]

BLOCKLEY

Bloccanleah 855, Blochelei DB. Blocca's forest glade or clearing. [p. name, lēah]

BOURNES GREEN

Bourne 1394. Stream by the green (running into the Frome). [burna]

BOURTON-ON-THE-HILL, BOURTON-ON-THE-WATER

Burchtun 714, Bortune DB. Fortified farmstead on the hill; the River Windrush flows through the village. [burh-tūn]

BOWBRIDGE

Bowbridge 1673. Arch bridge. [boga, brycg]

BOX

la Boxe 1260. (Place at) the box-tree. [box]

BOY'S GROVE
From the family of de Boys 14th c.

BRADLEY
Bradelege DB. Broad clearing. [brād, lēah]

BRAKE, THE
Thicket. [braec]

BRIMPSFIELD
Brymesfelde DB. Brēme's open land or land of bramble. [p. name or brēmel, feld]

BRIMSCOMBE
Bremescumbe 1306. Brēme's valley. [p. name, cumb]

BROAD CAMPDEN
Bradecampedene 1224. Valley with enclosures. Broad because it is spread out in comparison with Chipping Camden. [brād, camp, denu]

BROADWATER BOTTOM
Broadwater Bottom 1574. Broad stream. [brād, wæter]

BROADWAY
Bradanuuege 972, Bradeweia DB. (Place at) the broad way or road. [brād, weg]

Broadway Tower

BROADWELL

Bradewelle DB. Broad spring or stream. [brād, wella]

BROCKHAMPTON

Brochamtone 1166. Farmstead of dwellers by the brook. [brōc, hām, tūn]

BROTHERIDGE

Braderugge 1266. Broad ridge. [brād, hrycg]

BUCKLAND

Bochelande DB. Land granted by charter (granted to St Peters Gloucester by Kynred, king of the Mercians). [bōc-land]

BUCKLE WOOD

Bokholte 1340. Beech wood. [bōc, holt]

BULL BANK

Bulbanks 1622. Bank where bulls are kept. [bula, banke]

BUNNAGE

Bunadge 1598. Buna's escarpment. [p. name, ecg]

BURDON COURT

Burdenescourte 1450. From the Burdon family 13th c.

BURFORD

Beorgfeord 752, Bureford DB. Ford by a fortified place. [burh, ford]

BURLEIGH

Burleye 1248. Clearing near the fortification. [burh, lēah]

BUSSAGE

Bysrugge 1287. Bisa's ridge. [p.name, hrycg]

BUTTER ROW

Butterowe 1638. Archery butt. [butt, rāw]

BUTTS, THE

The Butts 1796. Abutting strip of land. [butte]

CAINSCROSS

Cain's Cross 1776. Probably from 18th c. surname.

CALCOT

Caldecote DB. Cold or cheerless cottage or shelter. [cald, cot]

CALLOWELL

Callowell Leaze 1639. Probably well in bare ground. [calu, wella]

CALMSDEN

Kalemundesdene 852. Calumund's valley. [p. name, denu]

CAMP, THE

The Camp 1779. Located between two long barrows.

CASSEY COMPTON

Cum tūn 962, Contone DB. Valley farmstead; affix from the Cassye family 16th c. [cumb, tūn]

CATSBRAIN TUMP

From ME 'catsbrain', ModE dialect 'rough clay mixed with stones' [tump]

CATSWOOD

Catewoode 1459. Wood of the wild cats. [catt, wudu]

CAUDLE GREEN

Caldewella 1155. Cold spring. [cald, wella]

CERNEY, NORTH & SOUTH

Cyrnea 852, Cernei DB. River Churn stream. [r. name, ēa]

CHALFORD

Chalforde ca. 1250. Chalk or limestone ford (part of the oolite beds). [cealc, ford]

CHARINGWORTH

Chevringavrde DB. Enclosure of Ceafor's people. [p. name, -inga-, worth]

CHARLTON ABBOTS & CHARLTON KINGS

Cerletone DB, Cherletone 1160. Farmstead of the freemen or peasants; Abbots relates to the ownership by Winchcombe Abbey; Kings because it was an ancient demesne of the Crown. [ceorl, tūn]

CHASTLETON

Ceastelton 777, Cestitone DB. Farmstead by the prehistoric camp. [ceastel, tūn]

CHEDWORTH

Ceddanwyrde 862, Cedeorde DB. Cedda's enclosure. [p. name, worth]

CHERINGTON

Cerintone DB. Village with a church. [cirice, tūn]

CHESCOMBE BOTTOM

Chescumbe 1227. Possibly valley where cheese is made. [cēse, cumb]

CHESSELS

Chestles 1732. Heap of stones (ancient site). [ceastel]

Market Hall, Chipping Camden

CHESTERTON

Cestertone DB. Farmstead near to or belonging to Cirencester. [ceaster, tūn]

CHIPPING CAMDEN

Campedene DB. Market place in the valley with enclosures. [cēping, camp, denu]

CHIPPING NORTON & OVER NORTON

Nortone DB, Spitulnorton 1217, Caldenorton ca. 1217, Overenorton 1302. North farmstead with a market; O. N. earlier 'cold north farmstead' the priory founded by Avelina, daughter of Ernulf de Hesding 11th c., had possibly the only hospital in Oxfordshire attached. ME *spital.* [cēping, north, tūn]

CIRENCESTER

Korinion ca. 150 (Ptolemy), Cironium ca. 650, Cirenceaster 9th c., Cyrneceaster ca. 1000, Cirecestre DB, Chiringecestre ca. 1270, Cycestre 1276, Circestre 14th c., Surencestre 1436, Cisetur 1453, Sissetur ca. 1500, Sussetour 16th c., Sisator 1685. Roman camp or fort of the *Cornovii* (this Celtic tribal name has possible links with Cornwall). [tribal name, ceaster]

CLAPTON ON THE HILL

Clopton 1171. Farmstead near a lump or hillock. [clop, tūn]

CLEEVE HILL

Clevehill 1564. Cliff hill (a prominent escarpment, c. 1000 ft). [clif, hyll]

St John the Baptist, Cirencester

CLIFFERDINE WOOD

Cliffordeam 1372. Homestead or meadow near the ford and steep bank. [clif, ford, hām]

CLIMPERWELL

Clymperwelle 1287. Possibly clotted well (source of the River Frome). [clympre, wella]

COATES

Cota 1175. The cottages. [cot]

COBBLER'S BOTTOM

Cobban Hyll, Cobban broc 1059. Cobba's bottom. [p. name]

COBERLEY

Culberlege DB. Cuthbert's glade or clearing. [p. name, lēah]

COCKLEFORD

Cockleford 1327. Ford where tares grow. [coccel, ford]

COCKSHOOT

Cockshoute launde 1400. Glade where woodcock were netted. [cocc-scīete]

COLD ASHTON

Escetone DB. Cold or exposed farmstead by the ash-tree. [cald, æsc, tūn]

COLDWELL BOTTOM

Caldewell 1494. Cold spring. [cald, wella]

COLESBOURNE

Colesburnan 9th c., Colesborne DB. Col's stream (from the River Churn). [p. name, burna]

COLN ROGERS, COLN ST ALDWYNS, COLN ST DENIS

Cunelgan 855, Colne DB, Culna Rogeri 13th c., Culna Sancti Aylwini 12th c., Colne Seint Denys 1287. Places by the River Coln. C.R. was given to Gloucester Abbey by Roger de Gloucester (d.1106); C. St A. probably named after the hermit St Ealdwine; C. St D. belonged to the church of St Denis at Paris in 1086. [r. name]

COMPTON ABDALE

Contone DB. Valley farmstead; affix possibly from the Apdale family. [cumb, tūn]

CONDICOTE

Cundicoton ca. 1052, Condicote DB. Cunda's cottage. [p. name, -ing, cot]

CONDICUP

Contercope Corner 1662. Possibly from French *contre-coup* 'cut back'.

CONYGRE LANE

Coney Gree lane 1775. Rabbit warren. [coninger]

CORNWELL

Cornewelle DB. Stream frequented by cranes or herons. [corn, wella]

COSCOMBE, UPPER & LOWER

Costicumb 1248. Costa's or Cōd's valley. [p. name, cumb]

COTSWOLDS

Codesuualt 12th c., Coteswaud 1250, Coddeswold 1269, Cotiswold 1440, Cottyswolde 1440, Cotssold 1541, Cottiswoldes 1543, Coteswowlde 1577, Cotswold 1592 (Shakespeare – Richard II), *Cotsall 1602* (Shakespeare – Merry Wives of Windsor). Possibly Cōd's high open land. [p. name, wald]

COWLEY

Kulege DB. Cow clearing. [cū, lēah]

CRANHAM

Craneham 12th c. Enclosure frequented by cranes or herons. [cran, ham]

CULKERTON

Culcortone DB. Culcere's (meaning 'the belcher') farmstead or farmstead with a waterhole. [p. name or culcor, tūn]

CUTSDEAN

Codestune DB. Possibly Cōd's valley or farmstead. [p. name, denu, tūn]

DAGLINGWORTH

Daglingworth ca. 1150. Enclosure of Dæggel's or Dæccel's people. [p. name, -ingas, worth]

DANEWAY

Denneway 1397. Road through the valley. [denu, weg]

DAYLESFORD

Dæglesford 718, Eilsford DB. Dægel's ford. [p. name, ford]

DEVIL'S CHIMNEY

Overlooking the quarried edge of Leckhampton Hill. According to legend, this tall pillar of limestone rises straight from hell.

DEVIL'S CHURCHYARD

Local folklore gives an account of an attempt to build a church here on an ancient pagan site. But whatever work was done in the day was destroyed at night by the Devil. The work was abandoned and the church built in Minchinhampton instead.

DIDBROOK

Duddebrok 1248. Dydda's brook. [p. name, brōc]

DIDMARTON

Dydimeretune 972, Dedemertone DB. Probably farmstead by Dydda's pool. [name, mere, tūn]

DITCHFORD-ON-FOSSE

Dicford 1052 & DB. Dyke ford over the Fosse way. [dīc, ford]

DONNINGTON

Doninton 1195. Farmstead associated with Dunna. [p. name, ing, tūn]

DORN

Dorene 964. From British *duro* 'gate', probably to a Roman fort.

DOUGHTON

Ductune 775. Duck farmstead. [dūce, tūn]

DOVER'S HILL

Named after Robert Dover (1582-1652) who instituted the 'Cotswold Olimpicks' here in 1612.

DOVEROW HILL

Dobensfeilde 1589. Possibly from a surname plus field. [felde]

DOWDESWELL, UPPER & LOWER

Dogodeswellan 8th c., *Dodesuuelle DB*. Dogod's spring or stream. [p. name, wella]

DRAYCOTT

Draicota 1208. Shed were a dray or sledge was kept. [dræg, cot]

DRIFFIELD

Drifelle DB. Stubble or dirt field. [drīf or drit, feld]

DUDBRIDGE

Duddebridge 13th c. Dudda's bridge. [p. name, brycg]

DUNKERSPOOL

Dunkirk home and mill 1839. Named from the siege of Dunkirk 1793.

DUNN'S HILL

From the family of Richard Dunne 1610.

DUNTISBOURNE ABBOTS, D. LEER, D. ROUSE

Duntesburne 1055, *Dantesborne DB*, *Tantesborne DB*, *Duntesburne DB*. Dunt's stream. D.A. affix is from the abbot of St Peter's, Gloucester; D.L. was held by the abbey of Lire in Normandy; D.R. was owned by Sir Roger le Rous 13th c. [p. name, burna]

DURSLEY

Dersilege DB. Dēorsig's glade or clearing. [p. name, lēah]

EAST END

Estende 1398. East end. [ēast, ende]

EASTCOMBE

Eastcombes 1633. Eastern valley. [ēast, cumb]

EASTINGTON

Esteueneston 1220. Ēadstūn's farmstead. [p. name, tūn]

EASTLEACH MARTIN & EASTLEACH TURVILLE

Lecche 862, Lec(c)e DB. East of the parish from the River Leach, church dedicated to St Martin; E. T. from the de Turville family who owned land here in the 13th c. [ēast, r. name]

EBRINGTON

Bristentune DB. Ēadbeorht's farmstead. [p. name, tūn]

EDDINGTON

Hedington 1241. Ēada's farmstead or hill. [p. name, ing, tūn or dūn]

EDGE

Egg 1300. Escarpment. [ecg]

EDGEWORTH

Egesworde DB. Ecgi's enclosure or enclosure on an edge or hillside. [p. name or ecg, worth]

ELKSTONE

Elchestane DB. Ēalāc's stone. [p. name, stān]

EVENLODE

Euulangelade 772, Eunilade DB. Eowla's river crossing. [p. name, gelād]

EWEN

Awilme 931. Spring or river source (source of Thames). [ǣ, welm]

EYCOTFIELD

Aicote DB. Cottage by the island or water-meadow. [ēg, cot]

EYFORD

Aiforde DB. Ford by an island or water-meadow. [ēg, ford]

FAIRFORD

Fagranforda 862, Fareforde DB. Clear ford. [fæger, ford]

FARMCOTE

Fernecote DB. Cottage among the ferns. [fearn, cot]

FARMINGTON

Tormentone DB. Farmstead near the pool where thorn trees grow. [thorn, mere, tūn]

FOLLY WOOD

Farley Gate 1830. Possibly fern clearing. [fearn, lēah, geat]

FORD

Forda 12th c. Ford (crosses the Windrush). [ford]

FOSSEBRIDGE

Foss Bridge 1779. Carries the Fosse Way over the River Coln. [foss]

FOUR SHIRE STONE

The Shire Stone 1607. Marks the spot where Gloucestershire, Oxfordshire, Warwickshire and Worcestershire once met.

FOXCOTE

Fuscote DB. Fox lair or den. [fox, cot]

FRAMPTON MANSELL

Frantone DB. Farmstead on River Frome; owned by the Mauncel family 13th – 14th c. [r. name, tūn]

FRANCE LYNCH

France Lynch 1779. Surname France and ridge. [hlinc]

FULBROOK

Fulebroc DB. Foul or dirty brook. [fūl, brōc]

FULFORD

Fuleford 1236. Foul or dirty ford. [fūl, ford]

FYFIELD

Fishide 12th c. Estate of five hides of land. [fīf, hīd]

GATCOMBE

Gatecumbe 1306. Valley gap between hills. [geat, cumb]

GOLDEN VALLEY

Golding 1779. Possibly due to wealth from local industries.

GOMM'S HOLE

Gomb's Hole 1774. From the surname Gomme.

GREET

Grete 12th c. Gravelly place. [grēote]

GRETTON

Gretona 1175. Farmstead near Greet. [tūn]

GUITING POWER, TEMPLE GUITING

Gythinge 814, Getinge DB. Rushing stream; G.P. affix refers to the le Poer family 13th c., T.G. refers to the fact that this was a preceptory of the Knights Templars 12th c. This was a cell of the head house of the Templars in London. [gyte, -ing]

HAILES

Heile DB. Possibly from a lost stream called Haylebrok 1256.

St Mary's, Temple Guiting

HALEBOURNE

The hale ground 1694. Nook of land by a stream. [halh, burna]

HAM

Hamme 1221. Water-meadow. [hamm]

HAM BUTTS

Ham-buts 1694. Strip of ploughed land abutting a meadow. [hamm, butte]

HAMPEN

Hagepinne DB. Hagena's pen or enclosure. [p. name, penn]

HAMPNETT

Hantone DB. High farmstead. [hēah, tūn]

HARESCOMBE

Hersecome DB. Hersa's valley. [p. name, cumb]

HARFORD

Heortford 8th c., Hvrford DB. Stag ford. [heorot, ford]

HARNHILL

Harehille DB. Grey hill or hare's hill. [hār, hyll]

HARTLEY BOTTOM & HILL

Hurtelegh 1221. Hart's glade. [heorot, lēah]

HATHEROP

Etherope DB. High outlying farmstead or secondary settlement. [hēah, throp]

HAWKESBURY UPTON

Upton 972. Hafoc's fortified place; affix upper farmstead. [p. name, burh, upp, tūn]

HAWKLEY WOOD

Hawkeleyswode 1461. Hawk's glade or clearing. [hafoc, lēah]

HAWLING

Hallinge DB. Settlement of the folk from Hallow or settlement of folk on the nook of land. [halh, -ingas]

HAYCROFT BOTTOM

Heycroft 1248. Hay croft. [hēg, croft]

HAZLETON

Hasedene DB. Farmstead where hazels grow. [hæsel, tūn]

HEAVENS, THE
Possibly 'heathens' (a heathen burial place?). [hæthen]

HEDGELEY BOTTOM
Edgley fields 1793. Hedge clearing. [hecg, lēah]

HETTY PEGLER'S TUMP
Formerly *The Barrow.* Small Neolithic hillock belonging to Edith Pegler, mentioned on a land deed 1683; from ModE dialect *tump.*

HIDCOTE BOYCE & HIDCOTE BERTRAM
Hudicota 716, Hedecote DB, Hidecote DB. Hydeca's cottage; Boyce from a feudal tenant Ernulf de Bosco 13th c.; Bertram possibly from tenant Philip Bertram 1221. [p. name, cot]

HILCOTE
Willecote DB. Possibly skinner's cottage. [hylda, cot]

HILLESLEY
Hilleah, Hildeslei DB. Hild's glade or clearing. [p. name, lēah]

HINCHWICK
Hunchewyk 1372. Hȳnci's dairy-farm. [p. name, wīc]

HOAR STONE
Hoar Stone 1713. Grey boundary stone. [hār, stān]

HOGLEY
Hoggeleye 13th c. Hog clearing. [hogg, lēah]

HOLWELL
Holewella 1189. Holy spring or stream. [hālig, wella]

HORCOTT
Horcote 13th c. Cottage in a dirty or muddy spot. [horu, cot]

HORNS, THE
The Horns 1777. Nook of land. [horn]

HORSLEY
Horselei DB. Horse clearing. [hors, lēah]

HUDDINKNOLL HILL
Huddinalls Hill 1400. Probably Hudda's hillock. [p. name, cnoll]

HUTNAGE
Hodockenasshe 1327. Probably Huddekin's ash-tree. [p. name, æsc]

Hetty Pegler's Tump, near Nympsfield

HYDE

Hida 1234. An estate of one hide (approx. 120 acres). [híd]

ICOMB

Iccacumb 781, Iacumbe DB. Icca's valley. [p. name, cumb]

IDBURY

Idberie DB. Ida's fortified place. [p. name, burh]

ILMINGTON

Ylmandun 978, Ilmedone DB. Elm-tree hill. [ylme, dūn]

IRELEY

Ireleyes 1586. Ira's clearing. [p.name, lēah]

JACKAMENT'S BOTTOM

Jockeyman's ground 1772. Probably from the surname Jackman.

KEMBLE

Kemele 682, Chemele DB. Possibly related to Welsh *cyfyl* 'border, brink, edge'.

KIFT'S GATE & KIFTSGATE COURT

Kyftesgate 1354. Possibly a gate or gap where meetings were held; there is a reference to an inquisition held in K.C. [cȳft, geat]

KILCOTT, LOWER & UPPER

Cyllincgcotan 10th c. Cottage associated with Cylla. [p. name, -ing, cot]

KILKENNY

A transferred Irish name after Kilkenny was captured by Cromwell in 1650 (from the Irish *Cill Chainnigh* meaning 'Church of Cainneach').

KINETON

Kinton 1191. Royal manor. [cyne, tūn]

KING'S STANLEY & LEONARD STANLEY

Stantone DB, Stanlege DB. King's stony clearing (from ownership by the Crown); L.S. from dedication of the church to St Leonard c. 1200. [stān, lēah]

KINGSCOTE

Chingescote DB. King's cottage. [cyning, cot]

KITLYE

Kitley 1609. Kite glade. [cȳta, lēah]

KITTS KNOB

Kites Nobb 1771. Possibly hill of the kites. [cȳta]

KNAPP, THE

Cuckold's Nap 1812. Perhaps a lovers' leap. [cnæpp]

KNAVE-IN-HOLE

Knave-in-all 1830. Probably youth in a secluded hollow or corner of land. [cnafa, halh]

KNEE BROOK, KNEE BRIDGE

Knee Brook 1830. Bend in the river (affluent of the Stour). [cnēow, brōc]

LADLECOMBE

Ledecome 1121. Possibly 'spoon-shaped hollow'. [hlædel, cumb]

LAMMAS, THE

Lammas orchard 1839. Possibly from the surname Lambert.

LANGLEY HILL

Langeleia 13th c. Long clearing on the hill. [lang, lēah, hyll]

LASBOROUGH

Lesseberge DB. Lesser or smaller barrow. [læssa, beorg]

LAVERTON

Lavertune 1160. Probably farmstead frequented by larks. [lāwerce or lāferce, tūn]

LECHLADE

Lecelade DB. Probably river crossing by the River Leach. [r. name, gelād]

LEIGHTERTON

Lettrintone 13th c. Farmstead where lettuce grows. [leahtric, tūn]

LEMINGTON, LOWER

Limentone DB. Probably farmstead near a river or stream called Limen (elm river), now lost. [r. name, tūn]

LIDCOMBE HILL

Lytcombe Hill 1540. Probably OE stream name from hlȳde meaning 'noisy one'. [r. name, cumb]

LISTERCOMBE BOTTOM

Lustercumb 1226. Dyer's valley or hollow. [litestere, cumb]

LITTLEWORTH

Litentvne DB. Little farmstead or enclosure (a common minor name in Gloucestershire, often a nickname for 'field of little value'). [lītel, tūn]

LONGBOROUGH

Langeberge DB. Long hill or barrow. [lang, beorg]

LONG STONE, THE

Has a local reputation for its healing powers. Also, like many of the prehistoric stones in the Avening area, inclined to go wandering at midnight.

LYNCHES, THE

Linchfield 1689. Ridge field. [hlinc, feld]

LYPIATT, MIDDLE

Lupeiate 1207. Gate in an animal enclosure where deer can leap over. [hlīep-geat]

MAUGERSBURY

Meilgaresbyri 714, Malgeresberie DB. Mæthelgār's fortified place. [p. name, burh]

MARSDEN HILL

Marisden 15th c. Boundary valley. [mære, denu]

MEON HILL

Mena DB. Probably from a British brook name meaning 'main' (it is located between two arms of a brook).

MEYSEY HAMPTON

Hantone DB. Home farm or homestead; affix from the de Meisi family, lords of the manor 12th c. [hām-tūn]

The Long Stone, near Minchinhampton

MICKLETON

Micclantun 1005, Muceltvne DB. Large or great farmstead. [micel, tūn]

MILTON END

Middletone 1327. Middle farmstead at the west end of town. [middel, tūn, ende]

MINCHINHAMPTON

Hantone DB. High farmstead of the nuns (owned by the nuns of the Trinity at Caen in Normandy 11th c.). [mynecen, hēah, tūn]

MISERDEN

Musardera 1186. Musard's manor (previously called Greenhampstead), owned by the French Musard (OFr meaning 'stupid') family 11–14th c. with OFr suffix *ere*.

MONKHAM WOOD

Monkscombe 1830. Monk's valley. [munuc, cumb]

MORETON-IN-MARSH

Mortun 714, Mortune DB. Farmstead in moorland or marshy ground; affix is a corruption of the lost Hennemarsh (marsh frequented by moorhens). [mōr, tūn, henn, mersc]

NAILSWORTH

Nailleswurd 1196. Nægel's enclosure. [p. name, worth]

NAUNTON

Niwetone DB. New farmstead. [nīwe, tūn]

NEATLEY

nataleahes c. 800. Probably wet-clearing. [næt, lēah]

NEEDLEHOLE

Needleshole 1814. Probably related to nearby Neatley. [hol]

NETHERCOTE

Nethercote 1192. Lower cottage. [neothera, cot]

NETHERTON

Neotheretun 780, Neotheretune DB. Lower farmstead. [neothera, tūn]

NETTLETON

Nettlecumb 1777. Nettle valley. [netele, cumb]

NEW TOWN

Newtone 1327. New village (a secondary settlement to Toddington) [nīwe, tūn]

NEWINGTON BAGPATH

Neueton DB, Baggepathe 1174. New farmstead; Bagpath was a separate estate, probably meaning 'badger's track'. [nīwe, tūn, bagga, pæth]

NIBLEY, NORTH

Hnibbanlege 940. Woodland clearing near the peak. [hnybba, lēah]

NORBURY

Norbury 1621. Northern stronghold. [north, burh]

NORCOTT

Nortcote DB. North cottage. [north, cot]

NORTHLEACH

Lecce DB. North of River Leach. [north, r. name]

St Peter and St Paul, Northleach

NORTHWICK PARK

Northwica 964. North dairy farm. [north, wīc]

NOTGROVE

Natangrafum 8th c., Nategrava DB. Wet grove or copse. [næt, grāf]

NOTTINGHAM HILL

Nottingham 1565. From the local Notyngham family, 15th c.

NUPEND

Upende 1639. Upper end of village. [upp, ende]

NUTTERSWOOD

Nutteswodd 1564. Nut wood. [hnutu, wudu]

NYMPSFIELD

Nymdesfelda 862, Nymdesfelde DB. Open land by the holy place or shrine from Celtic *nimet*. [feld]

OAKLEY WOOD

Achelie DB. Oak glade or clearing. [āc, lēah]

OAKRIDGE & OAKRIDGE LYNCH

Okerigge 1459. Oak-tree ridge bank. [āc, hrycg, hlinc]

ODDINGTON, UPPER & LOWER

Otintone DB. Farmstead associated with Otta. [p. name, ing, tūn]

OLDBURY ON THE HILL

Ealdanbyri 972, Aldeberie DB. Old fortication on the hill. [ald, burh]

OWDESWELL

Aldeswella 1191. Ald's spring or stream. [p. name, wella]

OWLPEN

Olepenne 12th c. Ol(l)a's enclosure. [p. name, penn]

OXPENS

Ox pen. [oxa, penn]

OZLEWORTH

Oslan wyrth 940, Osleuuorde DB. Ōsla's enclosure or enclosure frequented by blackbirds. [p. name or ōsle, worth]

PAGANHILL

Paggehull 12th c. Probably Pæcga's hill (this personal name comes from the OF name Paien 'the heathen'). [p. name, hyll]

PAINSWICK

Wiche DB. Dairy farm; later affix from Pain Fitzjohn, lord of the manor early 12th c. [wīc]

PARADISE

Paradys 1327. Not an uncommon name for a pleasant location.

St Mary's, Painswick

PAXFORD

Paxford 1208. Pæcc's ford. [p. name, ford]

PEGGLESWORTH

Peclesurde DB. Peccel's enclosure. [p. name, worth]

PEN HILL, LANE & WOOD

Penhill 1700. Probably from British *penno* meaning 'hill'.

PERROTT'S BROOK

Previously *Barrows brook 1777.*

PIEDMONT

Piedmont 1830. A transferred name from Italy.

PINKWELL

Pinkwell 1830. Finch well. [pinca, wella]

PINSWELL

Pindeswilla 680. Probably a spring from a dammed up pond. [pynd, wella]

PITCHCOMBE

Pitchenecumbe 13th c. Pincen's valley or pitch producing valley. [p. name or picen, cumb]

POOLE KEYNES

Pole 10th c., Pole DB. Pool; affix from Sir John Keynes, lord of the manor 14th c. [pōl]

POSTCOMBE

Posecumbes c. 800. Hollow valley. [posa, cumb]

POULTON

Pultune 855. Farmstead by the pool. [pull or pōl, tūn]

PRESTBURY

Preosdabyrig ca. 900, Presteberie DB. Priest's fortified place (from the priests of Cheltenham Minster 8th c.). [prēost, burh]

PRESTON

Prestitune DB. Priest's farmstead. [prēost, tūn]

PRINKNASH

Prynkenesse 1121. Princa's ash-tree (name from OE *princ* meaning 'blinking of an eye'). [p. name, æsc]

Near Winchcombe

PUCK PIT LANE
Puckpit 1815. Goblin haunted pit. [pūca, pytt]

PUCKHAM WOODS
Putcumbe 1274. Goblin valley. [pūca, cumb]

PUESDOWN
Peulesdon 1236. Peofel's down or hill. [p. name, dūn]

PYE MILL
Peomull 1383. Insect mill. [pēo, myln]

QUENINGTON
Quenintone DB. Cwēn's or women's farmstead. [p. name or cwene, -ing, tūn]

QUINTON, LOWER & UPPER
Quentone 848, Quenintone DB. Queen's farmstead. [cwēn, tūn]

RANDWICK
Randewiche 1121. Dependent farm on the border (outlying part of Standish). [rand, wīc]

RAPSGATE
Respigete DB. Probably a gate to an inquiry, denoting a place where public courts were held. [reps or resp, geat]

RAVENSGATE HILL

Ravensyate 1605. Hræfn's gate. [p. name, geat]

READY TOKEN

Ready Token 1796. A reference to an inn whose landlord robbed and murdered travellers, highwaymen were also active in this area. Perhaps some kind of token required to ensure a safe passage?

RENDCOMBE

Rindecumbe DB. Valley through which the Hrinde flows (a stream whose name means 'the pusher'). [r. name, cumb]

RISSINGTON, LITTLE, GREAT & WYCK

Risendune DB. Hill covered with brushwood; W.R. outlying farm or dairy-farm. [hrīsen, tūn, wīc]

RODBOROUGH

Roddanbeorg 896. Rodda's hill or upright pole on the hill. [p. name or rodde, beorg]

RODMARTON

Rodmertone DB. Farmstead by a reedy pool. [hrēod, mere, tūn]

ROEL

Rawelle c. 1050 & DB. Roebuck well or stream. [rā, wella]

ROOKSMOOR

Rookesmoore 1629. [hrōc, mōr]

RUSCOMBE

Ruscumbe 1567. Brushwood or rush valley. [hris or risc, cumb]

RYEFORD

Riford 1497. Ford for transporting the rye-harvest. [ryge, ford]

SAINT CHLOE

Sentodleag 8th c. Clearing made by burning. [senget, lēah]

SAINT PAUL'S EPISTLE

Paul Aposd. 1777, Epistle patch 1838. A barrow or mound near the parish boundary (Bradley Hundred), probably relates to 'beating the bounds' where a Bible reading took place.

SAINTBURY

Svinebury DB. Sæwine's fortified place. [p. name, burh]

SALFORD

Saltford 777, Salford DB. Ford over which salt is carried. [salt, ford]

SALMONSBURY

Sulmonnesburg 779. Ploughman's encampment. [sulh-mann, burh]

SALPERTON

Salpretune DB. Probably farmstead on a salt road (used by salt merchants). [salt, herepæth, tūn]

SAPPERTON

Sapertun ca. 1075, Sapletorne DB. Soapmaker's farmstead. [sāpere, tūn]

SCOTTSQUAR HILL

Soteshore 1102. Ridge of the steep hill of quarries. [scēot, ofer, quarriere]

SCRUBDITCH

Scrubditch 1773. Brushwood ditch or earthworks. [scrubb, dīc]

SEVEN SPRINGS

Seven Wells 1777. Source of the River Churn.

SEVENHAMPTON

Sevenhamtone DB. Village of seven homesteads. [seofan, hām-tūn]

SHEEPSCOMBE

Seppescombe 1292. Sheep valley. [scēap, cumb]

SHENBERROW HILL
Shunberrow Hill 1775. Possibly 'bright hill'. [scēne, beorg]

SHERBORNE
Scireburne DB. Bright, clear stream (Sherborne Brook is an affluent of the Windrush). [scīr, burna]

SHIPTON OLIFFE & SHIPTON SOLERS
Scipetune DB. Sheep farm; S.O. from the Olive family 14th c.; S.S. from the Solers family 13th c. [scēap, tūn]

SHORNCOTE
Schernecote DB. Cottage in a dirty or muddy place. [scearn, cot]

SIDDINGTON
Svidintone DB. (Land) south in the township (Cirencester). [sūth, in, tūn]

SLAD
The Slad 1779. Valley. [slæd]

SLAUGHTER, LOWER & UPPER
Sclostre DB. Slough or muddy place. [slōhtre]

SNOWSHILL
Snawesille DB. Hill of snow (where snow lay longest). [snāw, hyll]

SOUTHROP

Sudthropa 12th c. Southern outlying farmstead. [sūth, throp]

SPOONBED

Sponbedde 1327. Bed of wood chippings (as in building foundation). [spōn, bedd]

STANBOROUGH LANE

Stanberrow Down & Lane 1771. Stone barrow. [stān, beorg]

STANLEY PONTLARGE

Stanlege DB. Stony clearing or glade; affix from Robert de Pont del Arche 13th c. [stān, lēah]

STANTON

Stantone DB. Stony farmstead. [stān, tūn]

STANWAY

Stanwege 12th c. Stony road. [stān, weg]

STEAN BRIDGE

Stevenebridge 1248. Steven's bridge from a local's name. [brycg]

STINCHCOMBE

Styntescumbe 12th c. Valley frequented by the sand-piper or dunlin. [stint, cumb]

STOCKWELL

Stockwelle 1248. Well near tree-stump. [stocc, wella]

STONEHOUSE

Stanhuse DB. Stone house. [stān, hūs]

STOW-ON-THE-WOLD

Eduuardesstou DB. Holy place, hermitage or monastery (originally dedicated to the Church of St Edward 10th c.); later affix means high ground cleared of forest. [stōw, wald]

STOWELL

Stanuuelle DB. Stone well or spring. [stān, wella]

STRATTON

Stratone DB. Farmstead on Roman road. [strǣt, tūn]

STRETTON-ON-FOSSE

Stratone DB. Farmstead on a Roman road; affix is the Fosse Way. [strǣt, tūn]

STROUD

Strōd 1200. Marshy land overgrown with brushwood. [strōd]

St Mary's, Swinbrook

SUDELEY

Svedlege DB. South glade or clearing. [sūth, lēah]

SUDGROVE

Sodgrave 1248. South wood. [sūth, grāf]

SWELL, LOWER & UPPER

Swelle 706, Svelle DB. Swelling on rising ground or hill. [swelle]

SWINBROOK

Svinbroc DB. Pig brook. [swīn, brōc]

SYDE

Side DB. Hillside or slope. [sīde]

SYREFORD

Syersford 1779. Sigehere's ford. [p. name, ford]

TADDINGTON

Tateringctun 840, Tatintone DB. Tāthere's farmstead. [p. name, ing, tūn]

TARLTON

Torentune DB. Farmstead at the thorn clearing. [thorn, lēah, tūn]

TAYNTON

Tatinton DB. Farmstead associated with Tǣta. [p. name, -ing, tūn]

TETBURY & TETBURY UPTON

Tettanbyrg ca. 900, Teteberie DB, Uptone DB. Tette's fortified place; T.U. higher farmstead, above Tetbury [p. name, burh, upp, tūn]

THAMES HEAD BRIDGE

Thames Head Bridge 1777. Near the source of the Thames in Coates parish.

THEESCOMBE

Thieves Coomb 1830. Thieves valley. [thīof, cumb]

THICKLEATHER COPPICE

Thicke Leather 1692. Possibly 'dense reed-bed'. [thicce, lǣfer]

THORNDALE

Thornden 1327. Thorn-tree valley. [thorn, denu]

THROUGHAM

Troham DB. Probably a water course or conduit through a homestead or river bed (Holy Brook). [thrūh, hām or hamm]

THRUPP

Trop 1261. Outlying dependent farmstead. [throp]

TICKLESTONE

Ticklestone 1839. Unstable stone. [tikil, stān]

TILTUPS END

Tiltups Inn 1830. Possibly local dialect for 'covered wagon'.

TINGLE STONE, THE

Tangle-stone 1779. (Long barrow with a stone on top.) May be from ME *tingel* 'a nail', causing obstruction to the barrow entrance.

TODDINGTON

Todintun DB. Farmstead associated with Tuda. [p. name, -ing, tūn]

TODENHAM

Todanhom 804, Teodeham DB. Tēoda's water meadow or enclosed valley. [p. name, hamm]

TRESHAM

Tresham 972. Homestead among the brushwood. [trūs, hām]

TRILLIS

Trylles 1540. Probably a surname.

TRULLWELL

Trollwelle 1240. Possibly a well where strumpets were doused or submerged, from ModE *trowle* 'trollop or strumpet'. [wella]

TUNLEY

Tunleye 1220. Probably 'farmstead clearing'. [tūn, lēah]

TURKDEAN

Turcandene 8th c., Turchdene DB. Valley of the lost River Turce. [r. name, denu]

ULEY

Euulege DB. Yew-tree glade or clearing. [īw, lēah]

ULLENWOOD

Ullen Farm 1777. Possibly owls' wood. [ūle, wudu]

VATCH, THE

Vacchemylle 1459. Variation on ME *fecche* meaning 'mill grinding vetch'.

WASTE BOTTOM

Waste 1287. Wasteland. [waste]

WATLEDGE

Wadenegg 16th c. Wada's scarp. [p. name, ecg]

WATERLEY BOTTOM

Waterley 1571. Clearing by the stream (Doverle Brook). [wæter, lēah]

WATERMOOR

Watermoor 1709. Watery marshland. [wæter, mōr]

WESTCOTE

Westcote 1315. Westerly cottage. [west, cot]

WESTINGTON

Westington 1225. (Land) west in the village. [west, in, tūn]

WESTON SUBEDGE

Westone DB. West farmstead; affix means beneath (Latin *sub*) the edge or escarpment. [west, tūn, ecg]

WESTONBIRT

Westone DB. West farmstead; the le Bretts owned the manor 13th c. [west, tūn, p. name]

WESTWELL

Westwelle DB. Westerly well or spring. [west, wella]

WHITESHILL

Whitehill 1830. Modern name.

WHITTINGTON

Witetvne DB. Farmstead associated with Hwíta. [p. name, -ing, tūn]

WIGGOLD

Wyggewald 1109. Wicga's high open land. [p. name, wald]

WILLERSEY

Willerseye 8th c., Willersei DB. Wilheard's water-meadow or island. [p. name, ēg]

WILLIAMSTRIP PARK

Hetrop DB. High outlying farmstead; Willelm family owned the manor 11th c. [hēah, thorp]

WINCHCOMBE

Wincelcumbe 796, Wicecombe DB. Valley with a bend. [wincel, cumb]

WINDLASS HILL

Windsarse Hill 1772. Probably a particularly blustery passage squeezed between a pair of rotund, buttock like, hillocks. [wind, ears]

WINDRUSH

Wenric DB. From the River Windrush. [r. name]

WINSON

Winestune DB. Wine's farmstead. [p. name, tūn]

WINSTONE

Winestone DB. Wynna's stone. [p. name, stān]

WISHANGER

Wychangere 1221. Wooded hill-side near a marsh. [wisc, hangra]

WISTLEY HILL

Uisleag 759. Clearing near a swampy meadow. [wisc, lēah]

WITCOMBE, LITTLE & GREAT

Widecomesege 1121, Wyddecombe c.1300. Wide valley. [wīd, cumb]

WITHINGTON

Wudiandun 736, Widindune DB. Widia's hill. [p. name, tūn]

WITTANTREE

Wittingtree 1841. Possibly tree where councillors met. [wita, trēow]

WOEFULDANE BOTTOM

An unsubstantiated story tells of a battle here between Wolphgang the Saxon and Uffa the Dane. Or it may mean 'wolf meadow valley'. [wulf, hamm, denu]

WOODCHESTER

Uuduceastir 8th c., Widecestre DB. Roman camp in the wood. [wudu, ceaster]

WOODENHAM

Wodenham 1287. Probably Wōda's water-meadow. [p. name, hamm]

WOODMANCOTE

Wodemancote 1279. Woodman's cottage. [wudu, mann, cot]

WORTLEY

Wurtheleye ca. 1200. Clearing for growing plants and vegetables. [wyrt, lēah]

WOTTON-UNDER-EDGE

Wudutune 940, Vutune DB. Farmstead in the wood (beneath the Cotswold escarpment). [wudu, tūn]

YANWORTH

Janeworth ca. 1050, Teneurde DB. Gæna's enclosure or enclosure for lambs. [p. name or ēan, worth]

Chipping Camden

APPENDICES

APPENDIX 1

Places surrounding the Cotswolds

ASCOTT-UNDER-WYCHWOOD

Estcot 1220. Eastern cottage(s) near Wychwood forest. [ēast, cot]

BISHOP'S CLEEVE

Clife 8th c., Clive DB. (Place) at the cliff or bank; affix from possession by the Bishops of Worcester 9th-14th c. [clif]

BROCKWORTH

Brocowardinge DB. Enclosure by the brook (Horsbere Brook). [brōc, worth]

CARTERTON

A recent name, founded by William Carterton in 1901.

CHARLBURY

Ceorlingburh c.1000. Stronghold or fortified place associated with Ceorl. [p. name, -ing-, burh]

CHELTENHAM

Celtanhomme 803, Chinteneham DB. Possibly Celta's water-meadow (the river name Chelt is a backformation from the place-name). [p. name, hamm]

CHIPPING SODBURY

Soppanbyrig 9th c., Sopeberie DB. Soppa's fortified place; a market was added in 1218. [cēping, p. name, burh]

COMPTON, LONG & LITTLE

Cuntone DB, Cantone parva DB. Farmstead in a valley. Long C. because of its length; Latin *parva* means 'little'. [cumb, tūn]

CRICKLADE

Cracgelade 10th c., Crichelade DB. Possibly river crossing over the hill. [crȳc, gelād]

EVESHAM

Eveshomme 709, Evesham DB. Ēof's land in a river-bend. [p. name, hamm]

GLOUCESTER

Coloniae Glev 2nd c., Glowcestre DB. Roman town called Glevum (a Celtic word from Welsh *gloyw, gloew* and Irish *glé* 'bright'. [ceaster]

HONEYBOURNE

Huniburna 709, Huniburne DB. Places by the stream where honey is found. [hunig, burna]

LECKHAMPTON

Lechantone DB. Farmstead where leeks are grown. [lēac, hām-tūn]

MALMESBURY

Maldumesburg 685, Malmesberie DB. Maeldub's stronghold. [p. name, burh]

MILTON-UNDER-WYCHWOOD

Mideltone DB. Middle farmstead or estate near Wychwood forest. [p. middel, tūn]

ROLLRIGHT, LITTLE & GREAT

Rollandri DB. Possibly 'an estate with special legal rights belonging to Hrolla'. [p. name, landriht]

SHIPSTON-ON-STOUR

Scepuuæisctune c. 770, Scepwestun DB. Farmstead at a sheepwash; Stour is possibly a Celtic river name meaning 'the strong one'. [scēap-wæsc, tūn]

SHIPTON-UNDER-WYCHWOOD

Sciptone DB. Sheep farm near Wychwood Forest. [scēap, tūn]

WICKHAMFORD

Wicwona 709, Wiquene DB. Ford at a place called Wicwon, an old Celtic name possibly meaning 'plain in a wood'. [ford]

WITNEY

Wyttanige 969, Witenie DB. Witta's island or dry ground in marsh. [p. name, ēg]

WOODSTOCK

Wudestoce c.1000, Wodestoch DB. Woodland settlement. [wudu, stoc]

WYCHWOOD

Huiccewudu 840. Forest of the Hwicca tribe. [t. name, wudu]

Near Hazleton

APPENDIX 2

River and stream names

AVON

Afen 8th c. River. From the British *abonē.*

BLADEN

Bladon 7th c. Became known as the Evenlode in the 15th c.

CAM

Cambrigga 1200. Probably from Celtic *cambo* 'crooked'.

CHURN

Cyrnea c. 800. Possibly linked to the tribe of Cornovii (see Cirencester).

COLN

Cunuglae 8th c. Celtic river name of uncertain origin.

DOVERLE BROOK

Dofærlan 10th c. Possibly 'pure water' from British *dubro* 'water' and *glano* 'pure'.

DIKLER BROOK

Thickeleure 13th c. Thick reed-bed. [thicce, læfer]

EVENLODE

Euenlode 1577. Eowla's river-crossing. [p. name, gelād]

EWELME

æwylme 940. Source of a river. [ǣ-welm]

FROME

aqua de Frome 1248. Celtic river name from Primitive Welsh *frōm* meaning 'fair, fine, brisk'.

HAM BROOK

Hambroc 1221. Water meadow. [hamm]

HOLY BROOK

Hollowwell 1609. Holy stream or spring. [hālig, wella]

ISBOURNE

Esenburnen 8th c. Ēsa's stream. [p. name, burna]

KNEE BROOK

Knee Brook 1830. Knee shaped bend in the river. [cnēow, brōc]

LEACH

Lec 8th c. Stream flowing through boggy land. [læcc]

STOUR

Sture 8th c. Possibly a Celtic name for 'strong one'.

STROUD WATER

Strodewater 1475. Named from Stroud.

THAMES

Tamesis 51 BC (Caesar), Temis 688, Tamyse 931, Temese 999, Thamyse 1244, Tamese 1300. Possibly from Celtic root *tam* meaning 'dark'.

WINDRUSH

Uuenrisc 8th c. Possibly a Celtic compound from Welsh *gwyn* 'white' and Gaelic *riasg* 'fen'.

APPENDIX 3

Road names

AKEMAN STREET

Accemannestrete 12th c. Roman road from Bath to St Albans. Uncertain first element. [strǣt]

BUCKLE STREET

Buggilde stret 709. Roman road from Bidford on Avon through Weston Subedge, Snowshill, Temple Guiting, the Slaughters to Bourton on the Water. Burghild's street. [p. name, strǣt]

ERMIN STREET

Ermingestrete. Roman road from Silchester, through Cirencester, to Gloucester. Probably 'Roman road of the followers of Earna'. [p. name, -inga-, strǣt]

FOSSE WAY

Foss 779. Ditch way. Roman road from Lincoln to Bath, so called from having a prominent ditch, probably for defence purposes, on either side. [foss, weg]

ICKNIELD or RYKNILD STREET

Icenhylte 903. A continuation of Buckle Street (from Bourton-on-the-Water to Rotherham in Yorkshire). Meaning uncertain, possibly from the Iceni tribe.

PORTWAY

Porteweye 1293. Occurs several times in Gloucestershire. Denotes a road leading to an important town. [port, weg]

RIDGEWAY, RUDGEWAY

Name used of various roads throughout the Cotswolds, also known to archaeologists as the Jurassic Way. [hrycg, weg]

SALTWAY, SALTERSWAY

Sealt stræte 969, Salteresweie 1225. Applied to several routes across the Cotswolds (salt was an essential preservative for meat and fish). [salt, weg]

WELSH WAY

le Waweweye 14th c. Route used by Welsh drovers for their cattle, running from Fairford through Ready Token, Barnsley, Ampney Crucis and Duntisbourne Rouse. [Walh, weg]

WHITE WAY

A ridgeway running from Cirencester to Compton Abdale joining the Saltway which runs towards Winchcombe. Probably another name for a salt way. [hwit, weg]

The Saxon church of St Andrew's, Coln Rogers

BIBLIOGRAPHY &
FURTHER READING

BIBLIOGRAPHY

Cameron, K. *English Place Names*. Batsford 1996

Ekwall, E. *The Concise Oxford Dictionary of English Place-Names*. Oxford 4th ed. 1960

Gelling, M. *The Place-Names of Oxfordshire*. EPNS Cambridge 1953/54

Gelling, M. *Place-Names in the Landscape*. Dent 1984

Gelling, M. and Cole, A. *The Landscape of Place-Names*. Tyas 2000

Mills, A.D. *Dictionary of British Place-Names*. Oxford 2003

Smith, A.H. *English Place-Name Elements*. EPNS Cambridge 1956

Smith, A.H. *The Place-Names of Gloucestershire*. EPNS Cambridge 1964/65

FURTHER READING

Briggs, K.M. *The Folklore of the Cotswolds*. Batsford 1974

Brill, E. *Portrait of the Cotswolds*. Hale 1964

Crosher, G.R. *Along the Cotswold Ways*. Cassell 1976

Hadfield, C. and A.M. *The Cotswolds*. Batsford 1966

Hadfield, C. and A.M. (Ed.). *The Cotswolds: A New Study*. David & Charles 1973

Lewis, J.R. *Cotswold Villages*. Hale 1974

Massingham, H. J. *Cotswold Country*. Batsford 1937